As a Licensed Clinical Social Worker I realized that a lot of people are having challenges with identifying who they are. I wanted to create a journal that will help individuals discover who they are from the inside out. Learning to undo toxic behaviors is a process. It take dedication and commitment to yourself in order to change. Being able to tap inside your inner voice will allow you to be free and honest with challenges you are facing. Utilize this journal to help enhance the quality of your life and to be a better you.

MAKE MENTAL HEALTH A PRIORITY

BE YOU

CONTENTS

MONTHLY GOALS

Only you determine your destination

MONTH 1

MONTH 2

MONTH 3

MONTH 4

MONTHLY GOALS

Only you determine your destination

MONTH 5

MONTH 6

MONTH 7

MONTH 8

MONTHLY GOALS

Only you determine your destination

MONTH 9

MONTH 10

MONTH 11

MONTH 12

WHO ARE YOU

RENEWING SELF-WORTH

Summarize who you are today

_____

_____

_____

_____

_____

_____

_____

_____

_____

FORGIVENESS

MOVING FORWARD

Write down things you want to forgive yourself for

_____

_____

_____

_____

_____

_____

_____

_____

_____

MANIFEST

FUTURE GOALS

Be detail about your wants and needs

_____

_____

_____

_____

_____

_____

_____

_____

_____

NON-NEGOTIABLES

NO MORE COMPROMISING

Identify what you will no longer accept moving forward

_____

_____

_____

_____

_____

_____

_____

_____

_____

TRIGGERS

UNDERSTANDING YOUR EMOTIONS

What affects you mentally, emotionally, and spiritually

_____

_____

_____

_____

_____

_____

_____

_____

_____

_____

POSITIVE AFFIRMATION

DEFINE WHO YOU ARE

List positive statements about yourself

_____

_____

_____

_____

_____

_____

_____

_____

_____

Supportive People
who do I call when I need extra support

SPIRITUAL GUIDANCE

NON-JUDGEMENT TALKS

A PESON I CAN HAVE A GOOD TIME WITH

A PERON THAT WILL HOLD ME ACCOUNTABLE

EMERGENCY HOTLINE

POSITIVE SUPPORT

FAMILY&FRIENDS

Summarize how they impact your life

_____

_____

_____

_____

_____

_____

_____

_____

_____

MEDITATION

CLARITY

Clear you mind and write how you are feeling right now

_____

_____

_____

_____

_____

_____

_____

_____

_____

WHAT DO YOU LIKE AND DISLIKE

NEW YOU

Idenitfy changes that has occured with you

_____

_____

_____

_____

_____

_____

_____

_____

_____

SELF CARE

In the boxes, describe how you have been taking care of yourself physically and mentally

DAILY CHECK IN'S

Monday

How are you feeling today?

Tuesday

How are you feeling today?

Wednesday

Any progress?

Thursday

Have you faced any challanges today?

DAILY CHECK IN'S

Friday

How are you feeling today?

Saturday

How are you feeling today?

Sunday

Relax and Breathe today

Great Job you have accomplished another week on your own. Keep going! You got this!

week:	Date:

DAILY CHECK IN'S

Monday
How are you feeling today?

Tuesday
How are you feeling today?

Wednesday
Any progress?

Thursday
Have you faced any challanges today?

DAILY CHECK IN'S

Friday

How are you feeling today?

Saturday

How are you feeling today?

Sunday

Relax and Breathe today

Great Job you have accomplished another week on your own. Keep going! You got this!

DAILY CHECK IN'S

Monday

How are you feeling today?

Tuesday

How are you feeling today?

Wednesday

Any progress?

Thursday

Have you faced any challanges today?

DAILY CHECK IN'S

Friday

How are you feeling today?

Saturday

How are you feeling today?

Sunday

Relax and Breathe today

Great Job you have accomplished another week on your own. Keep going! You got this!

week:	Date:

DAILY CHECK IN'S

Monday
How are you feeling today?

Tuesday
How are you feeling today?

Wednesday
Any progress?

Thursday
Have you faced any challanges today?

DAILY CHECK IN'S

Friday

How are you feeling today?

Saturday

How are you feeling today?

Sunday

Relax and Breathe today

Great Job you have accomplished another week on your own. Keep going! You got this!

Brittany Rice is a Licensed Clinical Social Worker in Georgia. She is the founder and owner of Be You Counseling Services LLC. Brittany has been working in the field for over 15 years. Be You Counseling Services is a virtual mental health agency that provides services to adolescences, adults and the elderly.

Contact info:
Website: www.beyoucounselingservices.org
Emails: brice@beyoucounselingservices.org
Facebook: Be You Counseling Services LLC
Instagram: beyou_counselingservices.

www.ingramcontent.com/pod-product-compliance
Lightning Source LLC
Chambersburg PA
CBHW052009280526
45793CB00005B/907